Reflections: Words
From the Soul

# Reflections: Words From the Soul

Dan Babcock

The picture of the Morning Glory on the cover was taken while on
vacation in the Russian River Valley, Sonoma County, California.

ISBN: 0692875026
ISBN 13: 9780692875025
Library of Congress Control Number: 2017907128
Dan Babcock, Maple Grove, MN

# Introduction

WHY WAS THIS book written – Reflections: Words from the Soul? Looking deep inside my heart and soul, there are answers that seem to be right for me. My hope is these messages may bring a type of peace to others. It may strike a chord that helps to guide someone in a positive direction in their life. My desire is to spread positive energy, knowledge, and love wherever possible. We all know our world needs this – now more than ever.

This book has many short, easy to read chapters with a different sentiment in each one. You may read this book all the way through in one sitting. More likely, you will read a chapter or two and put it down and get busy with your hectic life. Two days, two weeks, two months, or even two years later you may pick it up again and read another chapter. The book is designed in this format for the reader. Each chapter has its own story. The hope is that you find comfort and positive feelings from the words you read in this book. If you are able to do that, my purpose for being here on this earth has been fulfilled. Thank you!

Lots of Love to all,

Dan Babcock

# Chapters

# CHAPTER 1

## Awareness

MANY PEOPLE GO through life on auto pilot. We let everything that happens around us occur – then we simply react, without even a thought. This lack of awareness limits not only our purpose in life, but also greatly limits our overall happiness.

When do people become most aware? Usually, just before or directly after losing something or someone. We take many things for granted if we are not aware. Some of these things are sight, hearing, touch, friends, a spouse, parents, food, shelter, health, or even life itself. It is often said that a person is most aware just before death.

How can we become more aware? Imagine yourself without something or someone that you currently have in your life. If you can truly do this, you will become immediately aware of the value. Awareness can only happen if we consciously look at everything around us. It takes mental discipline and focus – and after much practice, can become a natural habit. Awareness is one of the initial pre-requisites for a life filled with happiness!

# CHAPTER 2

## The Mirror

I GREW UP in a small town in north central Minnesota. The local sentiment was New York City was a busy place. People did not smile, were not polite, and were not happy. A few years back I went to New York for the first time. I realized how wrong this thinking was. Yes, it was busy. But as I walked down the busy street near Times Square, I made eye contact with and smiled at everyone I met. It was amazing how many wonderful smiles I received in return. My initial thought was, are these people reacting to me or are they just happy people? So the next two blocks, I changed my demeanor. I showed a scowl to all I met. I did not see one smile in return. People would either look away or return a bitter angry look. I realized the "mirror theory." Whatever we portray to others will nearly always come back to us.

*Smile at others and they will smile at you.*
*Frown at others and they will frown at you.*
*Take from others and they will take from you.*
*Give to others and they will give to you.*
*Hate others and they will hate you.*
*Love others and they will love you.*

If we show a negative attitude, we truly do have a negative impact on this world in which we live. If we show a positive attitude, we truly do have a positive impact on this world in which we live. Let the mirror be a positive reflection that shines back at you!

# CHAPTER 3

## Thriving

WHAT IS THRIVING? Thriving is growing or developing to higher levels than ever before. We all have the potential to thrive.

Traumatic incidents are part of our lives and happen every day. Loved ones pass away. People close to us are involved in accidents. We may lose our sight or hearing. Even a meaningful relationship we assumed would be there forever may not last. We may be diagnosed with a disease or become involved in any other catastrophic event. When a traumatic incident happens in a person's life, there are generally one of five things that occur.

1. The person may actually become so depressed they physically die.
2. The person will not physically die, but may emotionally die. They will simply go

through the motions for the remainder of their life.

3. The most common scenario is the person will become part of society again, but they will never return to the same person they were before the incident occurred.

4. The person will find their way back and continue their life on the similar path they had been on before the incident happened.

5. The person will come back and become even stronger than they were before the catastrophic event occurred in their life – this is thriving.

Every person has a unique grieving process and must complete this process before they move on with their life. After they go through their time to cope with the tragedy, the thriving person will see it as an opportunity to learn and grow. They will become stronger than they were before the incident occurred.

The first step to thriving is to be aware this is a possibility. A thriving person realizes that all of life is a learning experience. They continue to positively evolve from everything that happens to them throughout their entire life. Choose thriving and feel yourself grow!

# CHAPTER 4

## Generation Improvement

MANY TIMES WE hear the comment from the older generation, "That younger generation just doesn't get it." We all learn from age and experience – and sometimes we forget, we also had to find our own way once upon a time.

An important key to generation improvement is parents must be aware of their positive and negative traits. If we blindly go through the process of raising our children without this awareness, the negative cycle will continue from generation to generation.

Once we become aware of our positives and negatives, we can then communicate to our children about these traits. Some examples of positive traits are being hard-working, goal-oriented, patient, kind, or caring. Explain to our children how they may inherit these positive characteristics. More importantly, explain to our children the negative traits they may inherit. Examples of negative traits may be stubbornness, a bad temper, impatience, laziness, or a judging personality. It is not easy to admit we have these negative traits. By teaching our children what they may expect, we can help them break the cycle of negatives. As our children become parents, they can do the same to educate their children.

This is how we accomplish "Generation Improvement" in our world!

# CHAPTER 5

## Free Will

WE ARE ALL like snowflakes – each person's world is different from every other person's world.

Many people feel free will is simply having the option to choose which path to take when forks in the road appear to us. Free will is much deeper than this belief. Free will allows each individual the opportunity for their own perception to become their own reality. The human mind is amazingly strong – in fact so strong, we do not comprehend its immense power. The beliefs we hold and the thoughts we have in every aspect of our life actually become our life.

However, this can also be a curse to those who do not understand its meaning. If a person does not realize that their perception becomes their reality, life can become extremely miserable. Negative perceptions suddenly become a negative life. On the contrary, positive perceptions become a positive life. Having this knowledge allows us to feed off all the positive things that we perceive. It also gives us the option to use negative situations as valuable learning experiences. We can turn a negative into a positive, with just a flip-flop of our perception.

The gift of free will is one of the most majestic blessings we could ever receive!

# CHAPTER 6

## Past Life Regression

For those who have not heard of past life regression, it is a process using a hypnotic state to go back to a previous life in our subconscious memory. Reincarnation is common in many religious beliefs. There are many stories that seem to support this philosophy. Children have led their families to places they have never been in this lifetime and have been known to remember many vivid details with uncanny accuracy about the area. In other instances children have spoken of how they had died in a previous life. Scars have been found on the child's body or head in the same region relating directly to how their death may have occurred. Many people feel they have been here in a previous life.

There are those in psychology that are adept at bringing a person back to a possible past life using mild hypnosis. Much can be gained in our present life by revisiting the experiences of past lives. Current fears, anxieties, relationship issues, and even physical ailments have been healed for many who have done past life regressions.

Personally, I have learned valuable lessons from my past life regressions. In one life, I was an explorer in England in the 15th century. Although there was a lot of love surrounding me, in my early twenties, I left my girlfriend and family to become a seafaring explorer. My quest for adventure outweighed what I had in my life at home. I died at a young age in a storm at sea. From this experience, I learned we should not take the special things we have in our life for granted, the most special of these being love.

In another past life, I was a caveman living in a desolate rocky area. My mother at the time was killed by a wild animal when I was approximately eight years old. I lived for another twenty years on my own in the caves, doing anything to survive day after day. I saw no other people and died in my mid to late twenties of what seemed at the time to be old age. From this experience, I learned to appreciate ALL people in my current life.  You never know how much you take people for granted until you experience having absolutely no one around.

When I got back home, I scoffed at this silly idea of being a caveman.  It seemed so far-fetched to me, I could not believe it.  That night I had a vivid dream of a five digit number as bold as could be.  The number was 08420.  I thought nothing of the past life regression I had done the day before.  I thought to myself, hmm... selling products all over the U.S., maybe this could be a zip code on the East Coast of a company I should contact.  So I looked up this number on the internet.  I was surprised to find it was a zip code in Catalonia, Spain (which ironically, I did not even know had 5 digit zip codes).  Suddenly, I thought about my past life regression.  Could it be this had something to do with explorers at sea?  It seemed to me I was in England, but maybe it was Spain.  I dug deeper into this area in Spain and no mention was made of explorers.  But as I looked into the history of this area, it stated some of the oldest human bones ever found were dug up in the caves located in this area of Spain.  Suddenly, a rush of goose bumps appeared and the hair stood up on the back of my neck. Maybe being a caveman was not as odd as I initially thought.

Reincarnation – true or not true? Having an open mind to past life regression can be a great help in our everyday life to each and every one of us!

# CHAPTER 7

## Love and Fear

MANY PEOPLE THINK love and hate are pure opposites. I believe instead, love and fear are on the opposing ends of the emotional spectrum. With love, anything positive may be achieved. Fear, on the other hand, can cause paralysis in any given situation.

In many religions, God may be considered to be loved with all your heart, but at the same time ultimately feared. This seems to be a comparison of opposites. If you love anything with your whole heart, there should be no need to ever fear it. I do not believe the Source, which created all life, would ever want any living being to fear it.

From love comes joy, happiness, trust, and emotional elation. From fear comes anger, hate, jealousy, guilt, and many other negative emotions that can crush the human spirit.

Fear is not an easy emotion to rid ourselves of or to avoid. Looking at every situation through the eyes of love and gratitude can help immensely. We can choose which end of this spectrum to focus on. With practice, we can continually gravitate towards the side of love and away from fear.

Is your God a fearful God that you should be afraid of – or is your God an all-loving God that you should love with all your heart? I choose the loving God!

# CHAPTER 8

## Multiple Soul Mates

HAVE YOU EVER met a person you seem to have known or felt an immediate connection to, but know in this lifetime you have never met them before? This connection is not through words, but is a heart-to-heart or soul-to-soul feeling and knowing. Sometimes this happens to people early in life and the two may end up spending the rest of their days together on earth as marriage partners, and they say, "I have found my soul mate."

However, if we keep our heart and soul open, this feeling may occur multiple times in one lifetime. It is not limited by gender, as it can happen between any two people at anytime. We have a tendency to shy away from this if it happens more than once. The fear of societal judgments and potential intimate interaction will scare us away from this possible connection. A deeper soul trusts the feeling of love, instead of fear, in this situation.

This true unconditional love is felt deeply from soul-to-soul. It is the truest of loves as the ego is removed. Our wish is for the other person to experience only ultimate joy and happiness.

Once we have moved on from our earthly bodies – we will be with these soul mates again in the hereafter. There will be many souls we will associate with and finding them here on earth is a blessing. As soul mates, we can support each other, feed the positive energy back and forth, and grow together learning the lessons we are all here to learn. The peace of knowing you will be with these souls again is a wonderful feeling. Look for soul mates every day, for you never know when they will appear!

## CHAPTER 9

# Evolving Into Soul Mates

THERE ARE TIMES in our life when we meet someone, but do not feel the immediate "soul mate" connection. My wife and I met on a blind date 25 years ago. We liked each other a lot, but neither of us felt at first meeting, "Oh my goodness, this is the exact person I have been searching for all of my life." Over time, our love has become stronger and stronger every day. We are best friends and love each other very much. Our souls are now progressing along similar paths. We have become soul mates, but it was and still is an evolving process.

When we first meet someone, we may not feel an instant connection. After spending some time with them, we may truly get to know the person. As we drop our walls and defenses, we let others into our world and into our soul. At this point, we may feel a heart-to-heart or soul-to-soul connection that is deeper than anything we could have imagined.

When we stay open enough to allow these connections to develop, we find there are multiple opportunities to connect on a level as soul mates. While here on earth, our souls continue to learn and evolve. Soul evolution occurs at different rates and as we continue to meet people, we may align with them at any point. Keep your mind, heart, and soul open and you never know when you may begin evolving with a new soul that crosses your path!

# CHAPTER 10

## Coping Mechanisms

THE PATH OF life has many bumps along the way. Coping mechanisms are strategies that allow us to overcome these issues. They help us to regain emotional stability and happiness following a major unsettling event. Although many people feel these are only subconscious adaptations, it can be a conscious effort that allows us to cope and move on in a positive direction in our life.

The first conscious choice is to put the situation into a context of understanding that someone else has it worse off than us. This will help our emotional being to accept the issue at hand. A friend of mine was diagnosed with cancer and it was a life-changer for her and her husband. After going to the Mayo Clinic for treatment, they saw people with similar issues and others with even more difficult predicaments. They now knew they could deal with what was thrust upon them. They knew they were not alone in their battle and there were others who had an even tougher hill to climb. This was a huge step in allowing them to cope with their life changing event.

Another coping mechanism we can choose is to "see a light at the end of the tunnel." A loved one very near to us may pass away. Knowing we will be with them at some point for eternity is an excellent way to deal with this loss. It will not remove the sadness of missing them, but it will allow us to cope with the long-term pain and lessen the intensity of the emotional burden we feel.

The final coping mechanism is being aware of the fact that we are all here on earth to learn lessons. This type of understanding is helpful and allows our emotional depression to subside. We can then find the stability needed to carry on in our lives.

Coping mechanisms allow us to overcome the difficult times we are confronted with. It is important to consciously search for them, for they will help to get our life back on a positive track!

# CHAPTER 11

## "Got To" or "Get To"

WE OFTEN SAY and hear such comments as, "I've got to go to work" or "I've got to feed the dog" or "I've got to watch the kids" or "I've got to clean the house." "Got to" has a feeling of negativity and sounds like we are being forced to be responsible for doing something we do not want to do. In reality, if we look at these chores as blessings to be thankful for, then these jobs can become fun and satisfying.

How can we make this change? Simply by turning the "got to" into "get to." "I get to go to work and I am thankful I have a job." "I get to feed my dog and am lucky to have such a loving and faithful friend." "I get to watch the kids and am fortunate I was able to have children and a family." "I get to clean the house and I appreciate having a place to live, whereas many others are homeless."

Simply the feeling of appreciation will change the "got to" to "get to." When we get to do things, we feel joy and satisfaction while we are doing these things. What was once thought of as a burden, is now perceived as an opportunity and a wonderful gift. If happiness is something you strive for in your life, just turn your "got to" into "get to!"

# CHAPTER 12

## Testers

As we go through life, there will be many situations and people that will put us through tests. All of life is a learning experience and our greatest opportunities to learn and grow will come from these obstacles called "testers."

Sometimes the answer to the test is to battle until we overcome the issue at hand. Other times, after trying our best we still may not succeed. The answer this time is to learn that failure is a part of life and how to cope with failure. Another answer may be learning to walk away and save the time and energy that would have gone into a needless battle.

Not only are situations "testers", but people are put into our lives as "testers." We have heard it said, "He sure can test my patience." "Testers" allow us the opportunity to grow and learn patience, anger control, empathy, compassion, love, and many other positive attributes.

It is important for us to realize that "testers" may be a positive influence in our lives. At first impression, we may see "testers" as only having a negative impact on us. With a change of our perception we can learn and evolve more by paying attention to the "testers", instead of avoiding them. We must be able to ask ourselves, "What can I learn from this situation or this person?" Once we figure out the answer, we can apply it to our life and be prepared for the next "tester" to come along. "Testers" are a huge opportunity for growth and evolution on our life path!

# CHAPTER 13

## Heaven and Hell

WHAT IS HEAVEN? What is hell? These two questions have a multitude of answers when asked to the general public. I believe heaven is a place where love is the entire focus. If love was the number one priority of humankind, we would experience heaven on earth. As I perceive heaven and hell to be opposites, I feel hell is a place where love cannot be found. It is the absence of love. Fear and hate rule hell and it becomes the ultimate state of misery. Love and joy rule heaven and it becomes the ultimate state of utopia.

Can we find heaven on earth? Each person has their own answer to this question. Whenever I surround myself with love, I feel heaven on earth. Can we find hell on earth? Again, each person has their own answer to this question. Where love is absent and evil, fear, and hate are found, I believe hell is present.

As far as an afterlife, how could a God of love want any of his creatures to be in a place without love? God has given us a special gift that allows us to choose our preference. If you want to show love, be love, and experience love then your choice is heaven. If you decide not to show love, be love, or experience love then your choice is hell. I hope you choose heaven and your heaven is love!

# CHAPTER 14

## You be the Judge

I ONCE HEARD a story explaining how God would accept any human being who wanted to be a part of Him. God would not judge any creature on earth that was part of His creation.

A man had three children. He felt he knew who was good and evil and who should go to heaven and who should go to hell. God took the man aside and said to him, "I will let you be the judge and we will see how you do, but I will pick who you must judge." The man feeling very confident thought this would be easy and told God he would be happy to judge whomever God chose for him. God's next comment made the man's heart sink deeply. "The three people you must judge will be your children. Two of them may be allowed to enter heaven and one of them must go to hell for eternity." In tears, the man retracted his boast that he could easily judge. He said, "How could

I ever condemn one of my very own children to hell?  I cannot and will not do this."  Softly, God comforted him saying, "You will not have to do this, but now you know how I feel.  These are all my children on earth, and if they want to be with me, I will not condemn any one of them."

This is difficult for people to understand with all the evil that goes on in the world.  It does, however, put things into a very unique context.  We are all God's children. He will take any one of us who wants to be with Him.  Anyone who truly wants to be with the God of love will deeply try to show love and stay away from evil.  We do not know what is within the hearts of people and it is not our job to judge them.  Start by looking in the mirror. You can make a positive impact on this world by spreading love instead of judging others!

# CHAPTER 15

# Religion and Spirituality

RELIGION AND SPIRITUALITY may seem to be the same thing. I feel there is a difference between the two. Religion is created by humans and often consists of organized beliefs. It has man-made rules to follow in the worship of the God involved. Spirituality is a connection between each specific individual and that person's highest source that he/she believes in. Religion is an external belief system that a person follows, governed by what that person is told by an external force. Spirituality is a knowing or feeling that comes from within each individual's heart and soul. Although external forces may have an impact on a person's spirituality, the true decision made by that individual will come from a searching within.

Both religion and spirituality can be beneficial to the human race. Structured religion provides a strong foundation regarding ethics, morals, and "doing the right thing." It also provides an excellent support structure for people in time of need. However, religion may also create intense and extreme beliefs. This excessive intensity can lead to conflict, terrorism, killing, and war. Spirituality seems to be much more of an intimate or "one-on-one" relationship with the true source. Individuals may achieve internal peace and comfort through spirituality.

Although religion and spirituality are similar and may be synergistic, there is a difference between them. One or the other may be practiced. Or both may be practiced – side by side. There is no right or wrong answer regarding religion and spirituality. If you choose religion, spirituality, or both – they can be a terrific aide in helping you through your lifelong trek!

# CHAPTER 16

## Choices

ALL OF US have choices throughout our lifetime. We may not be able to control what happens to us or around us. However, we can always make a conscious choice that will determine our attitude regarding each situation. No external forces can stop us from making this choice.

We hear of the person who survives a tragedy through some of the toughest conditions. They were lost in the woods and survived many days against all odds. We hear about the prisoner who was tortured for days upon end, but still managed to live through the ordeal – where most people would have given up and died. How does this happen? These people have made internal choices to deal with what has been thrust upon them. They accept the current situation and choose to perceive the occurrence in a manner that allows them to push on.

Bad things happen every day. If we choose to look at each instance as an opportunity to learn something, we have then made an awesome choice. Turn the tables on misfortune and allow everything that happens to us to become a positive learning experience. Nobody can stop you from choosing this option. It will allow your life to be filled with joy and happiness and purpose. Choices are beautiful gifts we have all been given. We can use the power of choice every moment of our life!

# CHAPTER 17

## Negatives

LIFE IS FILLED with ups and downs. A good friend of mine has a saying that is a great philosophy to live by. He says, "It's never as good as it seems, and it's never as bad as it seems." With an attitude like this, it keeps a person on an even keel. You never get too high and you never get too low. Negative things happen to all of us in life – it is part of life. Realize that things will turn around. Look for those changes that will allow you to come out of your downward spiral or rut. If a person feels self pity and wallows in their misfortune when things are bad, they will remain in that down time much longer than needed. They begin to look for the next bad thing to occur and when searching for another negative, they will be sure to find it.

An attitude change can help us deal with the negative situation and allow us to move forward and out of the doldrums much quicker. Ask the question, "What can I learn from this occurrence?" Look at how this can become a positive step in the learning experience of life. Be happy with the opportunity to learn and evolve and move forward.

Another friend of mine had a great idea of how to get out of the negative rut. She would get a notepad and start writing all the positive things that she had in her life. Before she knew it, her negative mindset would automatically become a feeling of joy and good fortune. The blessings she had been taking for granted in her life had now become the focus of her attention and replaced her negative thoughts.

Negatives happen to all of us. Do what it takes to turn them around and find the positives in your perception. That perception will then become your positive reality!

# CHAPTER 18

## Positives

I WILL GO back to the same statement I made in the previous chapter to start this chapter. "It's never as good as it seems and it's never as bad as it seems." When positives show up in our life, we can react a couple different ways. Balance is the key. Some people will become giddy with happiness and have difficulty controlling their emotions. This is fine in the short term, but it can lead to the "roller coaster" effect. Once you come down from this high, you will crash hard. This causes emotional imbalance and is difficult for anybody to deal with. Others will downplay the positive occurrence and say "I don't deserve this good fortune." They feel guilty that they had a chance to experience this positive event in their life. In this case, they don't allow themselves the opportunity to receive any of the joy they deserve. Either of these excessive reactions to a positive experience can be detrimental to us.

Finding balance when something positive happens will help you in your life. Be humble and happy you have been chosen to experience this occurrence. Don't forget to show gratitude and give thanks to the universe when you are selected to experience something wonderful. Continue moving forward and allow more of these positives to show up in your life. They may start appearing much more frequently than you think!

# CHAPTER 19

## Attraction

VISUALIZATION, PERCEPTION, BELIEVING, and accepting are all parts of the process in attracting something you would like to have in your life. If you long for something, the first step is to meditate and visualize you already have the object you desire. How does it feel to have it? Put yourself in the position of already possessing the object and feel the emotions that go along with it.

Perceive how you will get what you are trying to attract. Relax quietly, and let it play out like a movie in your mind – knowing that your perception will become your reality.

Wanting something does not always produce it. If you tell your mind you want something, you may continue to want it and never get it. You must change your perception to having instead of wanting.

Believing is the key to achieving. If you do not believe, how can you achieve? Believing is not hoping or wishing. Believing is having the faith that what you are trying to attract will come to you.

Finally, accepting is a must. What you desire may not come in the timely manner you think it should. Maybe the timing is not right. Maybe what you desire is truly not best for you in the scope of your life path. Don't give up, but accept that things happen for the greater good in your life. We don't know the plan, but the plan always has a way of working out.

Visualize, perceive, and believe to achieve your desires. You will then attract them. Follow these steps and always learn to accept the results. You are setting yourself up for The Law of Attraction!

# CHAPTER 20

## *Evolution*

WHAT IS EVOLUTION? It is basically a change that takes place as time marches on. Change and evolution are inevitable. You hear the comment, "The only thing constant is change." That is so true. Those who accept change and adapt to change have a much better chance of finding joy and happiness in life. Those who constantly fight change will experience anger, fear, hate, and depression. They cannot control these changes that are happening every day.

Change or evolution can be a positive thing in our lives. We hear that God spoke to those who wrote books in the past and we should heed those writings. But why would God stop talking to people as the world continues to evolve and change? I believe God still speaks to us, more than we would ever know. We can continue to read books from writers that God continues to speak through. This

41

can help us in the fast-paced world that is changing at record speeds. If we pray and meditate, we can also find that God will speak directly to our heart and soul. The answers of how to deal with the changes taking place can be found within our heart and soul. It is a knowing we can obtain, if we just open up to it. Creative thoughts and ideas may come from external avenues, but knowing only comes from within. Knowing also continues to evolve and change from day to day. This is what promotes the growth of the human spirit.

Evolution is forever happening in our world. We need to embrace this concept and learn how to deal with it to the best of our ability. Allow yourself to accept and welcome external changes that are occurring. The lessons you learn and the internal growth you experience from evolution will be your reward!

# CHAPTER 21

## Giving

WHAT IS THE true measure of life? It is not what we accumulate over a lifetime, but what we give away over a lifetime that is the true measurement of our life.

When I was younger, I heard that if I would give to others, I would get tenfold or more in return. What you sow is what you reap. I thought to myself, "1 am going test this theory out." I began giving money to charities and waited patiently to get a large return. Every time I donated something I thought, "Just think how much I am going to get back for this one." The problem was, the harder I looked for the return, the harder it was to find. Then something changed. I gave money to someone I did not know at all, but realized they were very much in need. I got a big hug in return. This person told me, "You have no idea what a difference you have just made in my life." As a tear ran down his cheek he said, "You are an angel and God will bless you." At this point, I completely forgot about getting anything in return. My heart was melting. The love I felt in return from this person was the largest reward I could have ever received. I suddenly began giving because of the love and emotions I felt, instead of the desire to get something back. Soon after, my monetary return mysteriously began showing up. The less I looked for the return, the more naturally it flowed in my direction.

I started a tradition my past five times to Las Vegas. The last day of my trip, I go to the Walgreens by the Venetian. I pick up two dozen premade sandwiches and two dozen waters. I begin walking on the strip towards the MGM. I offer sandwiches and water to all the homeless people that I see along the way. What a rewarding feeling I get in return. These people have love in their hearts and are just waiting to say a kind word. They pass on wonderful blessings to me and I get many hugs filled with love and appreciation. By the time I reach Planet Hollywood, I usually run out of supplies. So back into the Walgreens I go and pick up one more load. By the time I reach the MGM I am physically exhausted, but am emotionally regenerated and feeling on top of the world. It is so rewarding!

When we think of giving, we often focus on the person receiving and how they feel. The reward the giver gets is just as fulfilling. Try giving - you will love it!

# CHAPTER 22

# Receiving

FROM MY PREVIOUS chapter and the story of handing out sandwiches and water on the strip in Vegas, I have an interesting story about receiving. Walking down the street, I ran into a homeless Sioux Indian woman originally from South Dakota. It was a very hot day and she welcomed the sandwich and water that I offered to her. On her wrist, was a mala bead bracelet that she had made when she was younger. After accepting the sandwich and water, she removed her bracelet and put it on my wrist, telling me this was her gift to me. Immediately, I felt I did not want to take this bracelet that meant so much to her. I declined, and told her "thank you," but I knew it meant a lot to her and I did not want to take it. She replied, "It will hurt me deeply if you do not accept it. You are giving love to all these people by handing out sandwiches and water. I know how good it makes you feel. If you don't accept this bracelet from me, as that is how I am giving love back to you – then you are rejecting my love. Please allow me to feel the wonderful feelings you receive as you give to all these people." Wow! I suddenly looked at this situation in a completely different light. I accepted the bracelet and with a big smile and a loving hug – we parted ways. I saw this woman again on a later trip. I was wearing the bracelet as I approached her. She recognized me and the bracelet immediately, and said, "I see you are still carrying my love." We both benefited deep in our soul from this encounter. Many times receiving is just as important as giving.

There is another situation I see happen between friends or family when a group goes out to eat together. The bill comes and one person adamantly takes the bill and says, "I've got this one." Too often, a disagreement ensues, as some of the others at the table want to pay for their share. What was meant to be a caring gesture may actually turn into hurt feelings and anger. Those who refuse to receive the gift of payment from the friend or family member are not allowing this person to feel the joy of giving. A great response in this situation is, "Thank you so much, that is so kind of you – I will take care of the next one when we get together."

Allow your friend or family member to get the full joy they are offering. Receive the gift with love and gratitude in return. For some it is harder to receive than give, but consider the situation and realize both giving and receiving can make the world a better place!

# CHAPTER 23

## God is Love

I WAS BROUGHT up as a Lutheran and attended church and Sunday School weekly while growing up. I learned a lot about the Bible and was always trying to figure out what the words and stories meant in my own way. One of the puzzles was the description of the trinity. God was the Father and Creator of the earth. Jesus was the Son of God that came to earth in human form to take away people's sins. The Holy Spirit was found within the human consciousness to guide us between right and wrong. The Bible stated these three separate entities were all one. How could that be?

At a very young age, I set out to determine my own answer to this question. As I read passages in the New Testament, I came up with an interesting thought. The Bible says that God is Love. If God, Jesus, and the Holy Spirit are all the same – maybe they are all Love, I pondered.

I tried a little experiment to test out my theory. I substituted the word "Love" in the Bible, wherever I found the words "God" or "Jesus" or "Holy Spirit." To me, this made perfect sense. God the Father, or "Love" created the world and watches over us. Jesus, or "Love" was sent to us in human form to teach us about love. The Holy Spirit, or "Love" lies within each of us and works to guide us to do what is right. As I have gotten older, I still live by this principal. I believe it is not only the case for Christianity, but is the true basis for nearly all religions.

What is God? To every person, this answer is unique, but yet it seems to be very similar. How can this be? I believe God is Love!

# CHAPTER 24

## *Intentions and Goals*

I HAVE HEARD it said that setting goals is the most important thing for a person to do if they want to become successful. I have also heard it said intentions are far more important than goals. It really depends on the perspective and priorities of the person making the statement. Both intentions and goals are important in a person's life. They may be considered synergistic. It does not have to be one or the other. It may be both.

Goals are an endpoint which we strive to achieve. An example of a goal would be to lose twenty pounds. Once we set a goal, we then come up with a strategy or action plan of how to reach the goal. The action plan is what we must do to get to the endpoint. An example of the action plan may be to not eat sugar, bread, or pasta while trying to reach our weight loss goal.

The intentions are the mindset we attempt to maintain as we follow our action plan towards the goal. An example of the intentions would be feeling good about ourselves and keeping a positive attitude while working towards our goal.

If we focus only on the goal, the task can become tedious. We lose the enjoyment of the journey on the way to the destination. If we focus on intentions along the path, our journey can be fun and rewarding. As odd as it may sound, yes – how we get there does matter.

Those who downplay goals will often state that failure to reach your goals can be crushing. Why set yourself up for this feeling, if there is potential for failure? Again, perception is the problem with this mindset. Failure to reach a goal should not be a negative consequence to the spirit or soul. The biggest learning experiences in life and soul growth often occur as a result of our failures. We learn what we did wrong and make a corrective action plan to do better on the next go-round. Yes, failure is an option and it is acceptable. The key is to learn from it and continue to practice consistent and never ending improvement.

Goals are step one and are good. The action plans are step two and are good. But remember to focus on the intentions you want to maintain – for they will fulfill your internal purpose and bring you joy and happiness on the way toward achieving your goals!

## CHAPTER 25

# Nature

OH, HOW I love nature. Plants and trees provide oxygen for people. I walk in the woods and breathe deeply. It is so refreshing. I feel the energy of the plants and trees. I absorb the oxygen they are putting out for me. It has a healing and re-energizing quality. On my walks, I see flowers, birds, and animals. I see water, grass, and the sky. I allow my perception to see all these things as miracles. The beauty is truly amazing.

What have I just done? I have made an escape from the fast-paced and hectic world in which we live. I have taken the time to use nature as a relaxer. I get back to my roots and re-connect with my soul.

I see the owl in the tree, the deer in the woods, the eagle soaring overhead, and the chickadee flitting through the branches off to my left. I spread loving energy to all of these and what does this do for me? It allows me to escape my problems, at least for a while. It allows me to recharge my internal batteries.

Often people are not in a physical location where they have immediate access to nature. But by taking a pause and thinking of a previous experience, or even an imagined one, you may transport your consciousness and feeling to this state of mind and get a quick recharge. When the real thing is not available, allow your mind to put you in a nature setting.

When I return to the fast-paced world, I have a new outlook. I am happy and have removed any negative attitudes that I had developed. My mind, body, and soul have been healed. Nature can do that for all of us. That is one of the reasons nature was created – please take advantage of it!

# CHAPTER 26

## Love Yourself

THIS BOOK HAS a lot of references to love. God is love. Give love to others. Receive love from others. Love nature and the positive things you find in your life. The most important place to start is loving yourself. It is impossible to send love to others if you don't first love yourself. This is where the basis for a happy life begins.

Easy to say, but how do we do this? As humans, we all make mistakes and it is easy to beat ourselves up for failing to live up to our own expectations. Most people are much tougher critics of themselves, than any other person on earth. It is natural. Loving yourself must first come with accepting who you are. We must realize that we are all on this journey together. Yet we each have our own path to take.

When you do something positive for others, allow yourself to feel good and let the love for yourself grow. Know you have a right to feel good about your accomplishments. In contrast, when you realize you have acted out in an improper way, make a correction. Accept the mistake you made and realize it may be painful. However, be proud you were aware enough to realize this error. Then make a change and let the love for yourself grow inside again. It takes practice, but it is worth the effort. Love is contagious and it starts within your own heart and can spread like wildfire, once you learn how to love yourself!

# CHAPTER 27

## Angel Numbers

HAVE YOU EVER had a three digit number show up repeatedly around you? It may be an angel number that has a deeper meaning than you think. You can look up the possible meaning of these numbers on the internet.

It is the middle of the night on a Saturday. I awaken and look over at my digital clock on the nightstand by my bed. The clock reads 3:33. I roll over and it feels like I fall asleep for what seems to be a half hour. I turn over and look at the clock again and it still shows 3:33. I think that sure seems strange. I must not have fallen asleep, like I thought. I close my eyes and this time I am quite sure I have slept for some time, as now it feels like morning is approaching. As I peer over at the clock, it still reads 3:33. Now I think, I must remember this and look up the number when I get up in the morning. This time I do go to sleep and wake up to the morning light. Of course, since I was half asleep when my middle of the night number occurrence happened, I completely forgot about it in the morning.

Later in the day, I get ready to go to the airport to pick up a business cohort coming in from the East Coast. He is going to be staying at our house for a couple days. The time is now 4:30 on Sunday afternoon. Before I leave, I must go to the downstairs bedroom where our guest will be staying and plug in the digital clock and set it. I plug it in and it says 12:00 when it first lights up. I hold the forward button down and it moves quickly towards the 4:30 time I must set it at. Suddenly, it stops and sticks at 3:33. Now I remember the night before and know I must look up this number, but I am late to the airport. So off I go and I will look this number up when I return home.

My guest and I stop and eat on the way home and then arrive at our house later that evening. I go to the computer to look up the number I have sticking in my head. I see an email from my brother who lives in Hawaii. It is March in Minnesota and it is cold. My brother has sent a joke about it being so cold my computer has frozen. On the picture of the computer, it says error number 333. I can't believe it! Now I hurry to look up what it says about this angel number. The site I find shows the number 333. It states the meaning of this number is that Angels are helping to assist me in my endeavors towards serving my divine life purpose and soul mission. They will guide me on my path and I should use my natural communicative and light-working skills to aid, assist, and serve others in a positive uplifting way. Hmmm, maybe it has something to do with my writing of this book guided by some very Special Sources.

Two weeks later my wife returns home from Florida after a business trip. We often listen to a relaxing music station on our television. She asks me the number of the station we always listen to? I tell her it is station 443. She says, "Wow that was my room number at the hotel in Florida. Let's look it up and see what it says about angel number 443." I assumed it would probably be something similar to what we had found before – stating this number is a positive sign in which Angels are watching over her and she is a light-worker also. To our surprise, it stated the person seeing this number is a hard worker, responsible, diligent, and very intense at reaching goals. Ironically, these are some of the strongest attributes my wife has as part of her personality. She works hard and feels immense responsibility to her job. This is a strength, but also a weakness as this trait becomes overwhelming for her. It is amazing how these two different numbers fit us both so closely. Are angel numbers fact or fiction? For us, they sure seem quite factual. Be prepared and you never know what angel numbers might show up for you!

# CHAPTER 28

## *Respect*

RESPECT IS ONE of the most important aspects of my life. My father was very adamant in teaching this to me when I was young. I am appreciative that he found it important to instill this quality in me. I have a different viewpoint than many. I hear people say, "I will give someone respect once they earn it and not until." However, I initially give any person I meet respect. Age, gender, race, or any other differences do not have an impact on my decision. I give everyone respect until they show me they don't deserve it or they show disrespect to others. This has been a positive trait for me throughout my entire life. Showing manners and respect will create a blessed and happy life for all of us. Disrespect will cause sorrow and unhappiness.

People are more willing to help you in a time of need if you are respectful. As the mirror theory goes, for those who show respect, they will be respected in return. For those who do not show respect, they will be disrespected in return.

Respect is extremely important in every aspect of your life. Respect your spouse or significant other and your odds are increased for a lasting relationship. Respect your friends and they will want to trust you and be there for you. Respect your coworkers and employers and you will find your job will go much smoother and chances for advancement will come much easier. Respect other family members and the bond will become stronger between you. Make the consistent effort at showing respect and you will be rewarded throughout your entire lifetime!

# CHAPTER 29

## Appreciation

APPRECIATION IS A key towards experiencing a life filled with happiness. The human race is filled with wants and desires of what we don't have, instead of what we do have. Lack of appreciation leads to jealousy, greed, anger, and hate. We become jealous of what others have, that we do not. We get a taste of something good and instead of savoring it and appreciating it our greed kicks in. We need more, more, more. We see a neighbor or coworker with something we wish we had and we feel anger, jealousy, and hatred towards this person.

We need to change our perception to be thankful for what we possess. How do we do this? If you are having trouble finding positives in your life, consider making a list or a gratitude journal. Every morning or evening sit quietly and write down the things that you appreciate. It doesn't have to be massive items. They can be as basic as walking, talking, the sun, rain, family, friends, your house, pets, other human beings, or just being alive. You will be surprised at the size of your list as you continue to jot down more and more items. After making this list on a continual basis, your thought process will start changing and you will begin recognizing things to appreciate. They will start appearing more frequently than you can believe. It will become a great habit which will make your life more enjoyable.

Next, start showing appreciation to those around you. What feels better than being appreciated by others? Monetary rewards are nice, but true appreciation goes right to the heart. It is a two way street. As you begin appreciating others, they will begin appreciating you. Just the words, "thank you" go a long way and can mean the world to someone. Give appreciation a try – you and those around you will like it!

# CHAPTER 30

## Death

THE FEAR AND sadness of death can be intense and overwhelming. When someone close to us dies, our heart will literally hurt. Chakras are energy points or nodes found in the body. There are seven chakras in the human body. The fourth chakra is the heart chakra. It is the center of our physical body and the source of our love. It is no wonder our pain originates from this area. Some people never get over this pain and it has a negative impact on their life from that point forward.

How can we try and lessen this pain we feel? How can we cope and move on with our life? How can we allow death to not have such a long lasting emotional impact on us? The first step is acceptance. Everyone will die. Accepting this fact is important. Do not suppress the pain you feel. This is natural and it is okay. Each and every one of us has a grieving process we must complete. The release of emotions during this grieving process is both emotionally and physically positive for the body and soul.

Once time has passed, the pain should begin to lessen. If it does not slowly ease up, life can become sad and dark. Faith is key in allowing us to deal with death. Faith in the afterlife will help us in this time of sadness. If we believe that the human body has ended, but the energy of the soul has moved on to another dimension, we can then change our thought process. Our human side will always miss the experience of the senses we had felt with this person. We know we will never be able to hug them again. Our soul, however, can rejoice. Our faith needs to be strong enough to believe the person's energy moves on to the next level through their soul. There is a great song by Diamond Rio called, "God Only Cries." This song is excellent in helping us cope with death and will most likely bring a tear to the eye. It tells of all the Angels with a smile on their face, because this person who died is in a better place. God is crying, not for the one who died, but for the living. They must carry on and are still so far from home. With faith, we can accept death from the side of love, instead of from the side of fear.

Another option is the assistance of a good medium. A medium has the ability to connect to the spirit dimension. Your loved one may come through and have messages for you. For some people this is quite far out and difficult to believe. But, if the pain will not go away, what is keeping you from trying something to help the situation? Many people have tried this option and it has allowed them to find peace and happiness. There are some so-called mediums that are out to scam you and take your money. There are also credible mediums that are truly gifted and have a unique ability to help you. Make sure to find one that has been recommended or has a few good references.

Finally, be open to looking for signs from the other side. Be aware of your surroundings and you may be pleasantly surprised at what might show up. A butterfly may come and land on you while you are thinking of your loved one. A television or radio may turn on without anyone near it. A number that had a special meaning to your loved one may show up in the oddest place. These coincidences can give us shots of emotional energy, peace, and love.

There is a positive side to death. Only you can change your perception to look at death from this viewpoint. Make this choice and it will help you as you travel on your path of life!

# CHAPTER 31

## Pets

THERE ARE FEW therapies that have the impact pets can have on our heart and soul. I have seen pets in a nursing care center lift the spirits of those who have not shown emotions for a long time. I have seen pets get a baby or toddler to begin giggling without end. Why is this? It happens because pets have a special type of unconditional love rarely found in people. We can learn a lot from this unconditional love that pets offer.

Remember to give love back to your pets. When you come home from work and they run and jump on you, it is because they love you. It is not because they want to get your pants or dress dirty. When they bark because they hear a noise outside, they are not trying to get on your nerves. They love you and are trying to let you know they would do anything to protect you. When you get ready to leave the house and they whine and hang on your leg, they are not trying to be a pest. They know you are leaving and will miss you so much it hurts them inside. When they get elderly, they still love you just as much as when they were a puppy. Give them love in return – they need it. Please remember these things and always let your pets know you love them.

Pets are a valuable part of our society – treat them with respect and love. And yes, I believe after our pets have passed away, we will see them again – for how can that type of unconditional love be kept out of heaven?

# CHAPTER 32

## *Ego*

HUMANS ARE FILLED with ego. The soul does not have an ego. Ego is developed from the day we are born and changes every day. It is how we see ourselves. Ego is based on what we have. Ego is based on what we do. Ego is what we think others think of us (our perceived reputation). Our ego is what keeps us separate from all others and separate from God.

Without awareness, our ego will grow until it controls our life. This causes us to judge others. We look at people or actions that happen around us and we think these things are either good or bad. That is our ego – judging. How can we work on suppressing the ego, so we judge less? We must first be aware of how often we judge throughout a day. If we were to track this, it would be mind boggling. Human nature allows the ego to judge everything that enters the mind. Is it good or bad?

Do we like it or not? The mind has a habit of asking these questions. The ego then jumps in with the answer, before we even have time to rationalize what is happening.

If we realize this is how our mind works, we can consciously start making minor changes to let go of our ego. When our mind sees something, relax and realize "it is what it is." It is neither good nor bad. It is simply an occurrence and we do not need to judge it. Practice this daily and the ego will begin to dissipate. Another practice to help relax the ego is giving to others. Every time we give, we are taking what we have (which is part of what our ego is made up of) and letting it go. We begin to see others as ourselves. We see everything, including God, as one. From this viewpoint, the ego is diminished. The closer we get to being one with everything around us, the less anxiety and fear we feel every day of our life. As we reduce our self-made ego, our life becomes easier and more relaxing. We are working our way back to the soul, from which we came. Remove the ego and let happiness and joy move to the forefront of your life!

# CHAPTER 33

## *Remembering*

WHEN WE COME into this world there seem to be thoughts in our mind that have been instilled from somewhere in our past. The soul has become incarnated as a human being. There are signs of past dimensions lodged within us.

Children may speak of past lives or imaginary friends they are convinced are real. The natural reaction of most parents is to silence this immediately. There is a fear of not fitting in with society. We are adept at putting these children's thoughts to rest. Usually by about three or four years old, the child begins to forget the things they would bring up in their earlier days. Could these memories that children are telling us be true? Could they have lived past lives? Could their imaginary friends be Angels or positive beings from the other side helping them assimilate to this new world?

We really do not have any factual evidence to prove one way or the other.

Is it possible for us to remember these things in our older years? The brain has much that is untapped and unknown. Through mild hypnosis or meditation, it seems some of these thoughts and memories can come back to certain people. They remember things that are not in this life, but where did these memories come from?

If we can remember occurrences before our lifetime, is there anything we can learn from this remembering? Some of these memories may help to put our mind and soul at ease. It reminds us that we are here for a reason. We are each fulfilling our own special purpose. Remembering helps us to learn the lessons we were meant to learn and allows our soul to grow!

# CHAPTER 34

## Selecting our Life

SOME PEOPLE BELIEVE our life has been pre-selected and our entire life has been scripted for us. We have no control over what happens in our lifetime. Others believe we had a large part in selecting our life. We may have selected where we were born. We may have chosen our parents and even our siblings. They may have also been involved in selecting us. This is an interesting thought to ponder. How much of our life is fate and how much is pre-determined? How much of our life is choices? Is it possible all of our life is choices and nothing has been predetermined?

The answers are for each of us to determine on our own. We are all here on a unique and special path. There is a starting point to our human life which is birth. There is an ending point which is death. Throughout our life, we are given choices. Our path may vary from time to time. We are here to learn the lessons we need to work on. Be open to what comes to us and realize everything happens for a reason. Ask these question at every turn. "What can we learn from this? How can we make improvements in our life from this most recent occurrence"?

The biggest question is not asking if our life has been pre-selected or not. More importantly, are we making the most of this life path we are on? Are we learning and evolving and growing along the way? I hope your answer is – "Yes". If it is, the feeling of fulfillment you will experience is the well deserved reward on the path you travel!

# CHAPTER 35

## Ted Comes to Visit

I HAD ALWAYS gotten along well with my father-in-law. He had a successful dairy farm in Minnesota, where he raised 11 children – my wife being eighth of the bunch. Ted was not an emotional father, but he provided very well for his family. The kids worked hard on the farm while going to school and were all a big part of the success. Putting in long hours, sometimes it was tough on the children at a young age. When Ted reached retirement years, the farm was taken over by the eldest son, and Ted and his wife Christine, moved to town.

The farm was in Ted's blood. Nearly every day, he made the drive out to the farm. He would help his son with the chores and other farm work. This continued for quite some time. Then one day while out on the farm, Ted suddenly passed away. It was unexpected and rough on the family, but he was right where he would have wanted to be on his last day. I am sure of that.

It was a Friday morning and Ted had been deceased for about two years. I got up to shower at home at around 8:30 am. Suddenly, out of nowhere I felt the presence of my father-in-law. I didn't see him, but I knew he was there. I wasn't afraid. I was just greatly surprised. "Ted", I said aloud, "what do you want?" In my heart, I felt the following comments. "Tell your wife I am sorry I did not give her the emotional support she longed for. I am with her in her travels and I love her very much. I should have told her so. Please give her a big hug and tell her it is from me." Then he was gone.

After getting out of the shower, I got dressed and immediately called my wife at work. She seemed to be more emotional than usual, and before I began the story of my morning experience, she needed to tell me something. A strange feeling occurred that she had never experienced before. She said, "I don't know why, but this morning I forgave my father." I was shocked as it seemed Ted's spirit had been busy that morning. I told her my story and we knew something very special had just happened to both of us.

Needless to say, when my wife arrived home from work that evening I gave her a big hug. It was very emotional and it felt awesome. Why did Ted pick me to come visit from the other side? I don't know. Maybe because I was open enough to listen. Always keep an open mind. You never know what amazing miracles could happen in your life!

# CHAPTER 36

## Jealousy

JEALOUSY IS A difficult emotion to understand. It arouses some of the most uncontrollable anger. What is the core reason for jealousy? If we dig deep enough, jealousy is based out of some type of fear. It can be the fear of losing somebody we love. It can be the fear of not having what the neighbors have. Our ego suffers with our lack of material possessions we have, in comparison to what others may have. It can be the fear of not being able to perform at the level someone else can perform. We may then feel we are not viewed the same way this other person is viewed, and our reputation suffers. In reality, jealousy is not about the other person, but instead it is about our own perceived shortcomings.

Society has reinforced the emotion of jealousy. It claims we must be "better than the next guy."

Or society pushes the "win at all costs" view. Then our winners are treated as heroes.

What can we do to avoid feelings of jealousy? Let's start with jealousy as it appears in a relationship. We see the one we care about having a good time with someone else. If we unconditionally love this person, we would see them being happy, and in turn be glad for them. How we view the situation makes all the difference in the world and it depends on our definition of true and unconditional love.

Here is another common act of jealousy. A spouse or significant other has an opportunity to do something special. A husband has an opportunity to go on a golfing trip for the weekend with his friends. A wife has a chance to have a weekend out of town with her girlfriends. They consult the other person, and jealousy rears its ugly head. We hear the comment, "Why would you do that without me?" Or one will say, "Sure, I have to stay home and watch the kids, while you go have fun?" True love does not promote jealousy. True love feels only joy and appreciation for the one we love. We are pleased when the one we love has an opportunity to experience happiness.

Unconditional love promotes feelings of joy and not jealousy. We are happy for the neighbor who gets the new car. We are happy for the co-worker that gets the job promotion or raise. Praise and appreciation are shown to a friend who can do something special that no one else can do. Let your love be stronger than your emotion of jealousy and everyone will benefit, including you!

# CHAPTER 37

## *Guilt*

GUILT CAN HANG over a person like a dark cloud bringing feelings of sadness and depression that seem to never end. Guilt has been used for years to control people. Parents consistently use guilt to get a child to behave in a certain way. They use guilt to stop the child from doing things they wish the child would not do. We hear comments such as "What would your father think?" "What would your mother think?" "If Santa knows you are doing that, he won't bring you presents this year."

Our government, media, and religions use guilt to get people to act the way they want them to act. "What would our founding fathers think about this?" "If you do that you will go to hell." "What would God think, if he knew what you were doing?"

We still need to admit when we make mistakes. We must be aware when we have done something that does not live up to our morals, ethics, or values. However, the key is to realize the error. Then make a change or improvement. First, we perform an action. Next, we learn from our action. Finally we must make the positive changes and move on.

It is not healthy to allow the emotion of guilt to dwell inside us for any extended period of time. Everyone makes mistakes in life. Hanging onto mistakes will take a negative toll on our well being. Use mistakes as a learning tool and make positive changes from them. Moving forward without the added stress of guilt will result in contentment and peace in our life!

# CHAPTER 38

## *Forgiveness*

HOLDING A GRUDGE or personal vendetta towards
another human being is all too common in our
world.  The person holding the grudge will easily justify the reason for not forgiving their enemy.
"They don't deserve to be forgiven after what they
have done," is the common statement.  The one
who refuses to forgive is the one who pays the long
term price for this action.  A wall is built within
this person's heart and contained within this wall
is hurt, bad feelings, and anger.  It is downright
miserable.

The one who benefits most is the one who does
the forgiving – not the forgiven.  A huge weight
is lifted from a person when they decide to forgive another person.  The negative energy that has
been bottled up inside now is set free to escape
and the relief is fantastic.

One of the hardest things to do is to forgive yourself. Self forgiveness is a key to achieving internal peace and providing comfort to the soul. We have a tendency to beat ourselves up for things we could have or should have done differently. When we refuse to forgive ourselves, our self esteem will be shaken. This leads to feelings of sadness and depression. It takes a strong effort to change this thought process, but forgiving yourself will help you follow a more enjoyable path in life.

What is more important to you, pride or forgiveness? The ego will always make sure that pride wins this battle. Be aware of this and put your ego in check. Let forgiveness be more important than pride. You will be a much happier person if this can be achieved!

# CHAPTER 39

## Joy

JOY IS ONE of the most rewarding feelings a human can experience. Those who are filled with joy have a good life. It is contagious and others love to be around these people. How do these people experience joy throughout their life?

Choosing how to look at things around us is the catalyst for a joyous life. Search for the positive things in all that we see. Yes, sometimes it is difficult when we don't get our way. We see so much negativity happening in our world. For many of these situations we can have no impact on what is happening. It is out of our control. But we do have complete control over how we choose to react and deal with the situation.

The more we search for positives, the easier they are to find and more frequently they begin to appear. When they do appear, remember to show gratitude and be thankful. Every time we give thanks, we experience a feeling of joy. Gratitude and joy go hand in hand. Something else that brings immediate joy is a smile. It is impossible to smile and not have a feeling of joy that stems from the heart.

Seeing positives, showing gratitude and putting on a smile will bring you joy. This joy that you feel will become contagious and will make the entire world a better place!

# CHAPTER 40

# Empathy and Compassion

EMPATHY IS TAKING on the feelings of another person or group of people. Some people are empaths and do not understand what is happening to them. Have you ever walked into a room and felt a sad or negative energy being given off by someone in the room? Or have you ever seen someone get hurt, and suddenly feel pain yourself? Or has your stomach hurt after seeing a tragic incident? These are signs of empathy.

Empathy is a touching and caring quality. It can however, be extremely overwhelming to take on other people's feelings. It may be confusing, whether these feelings are your own or if they may be somebody else's feelings that have worked their way inside of you. Strange as it may seem, you do have the ability to protect yourself from other people's feelings that could invade your space. Through meditation, you can imagine a brilliant white or gold light surrounding you. Focus and believe that this light will only allow in what is good. Negative feelings and other thoughts will be kept at bay by this protective light. If you think other people's feelings are negatively affecting you, try this meditation technique. Still continue to allow the empathy you feel toward others to soften your heart.

Compassion is very similar. Compassion allows you to feel sorry for others that are less fortunate than you. Compassion allows you to deal with others that you do not understand. You may not know why someone does something or acts a certain way. However, if you put yourself in their shoes, you may then be able to understand the other person's actions. If what another person does goes totally against your beliefs, instead of getting angry and upset at this person, you can show them compassion. Realize that what they are doing has a negative consequence for them. Deep down they are suffering and are extremely miserable. Be thankful you are not going through what they are going through. This does not mean anyone's actions are to be condoned. It means you can still feel love and caring for everyone – due to compassion. Compassion can make your life less stressful and much more comfortable when dealing with people on a daily basis!

# CHAPTER 41

## Patience

THE WORLD WE live in today moves at an unbeliev-able pace. Everyone seems to be in a hurry. People are late for work, horns are honking on the busy city streets, and everyone seems to be in everybody else's way. Is this a good thing for our world? Is this a good thing for each of us as human beings?

Patience goes a long way in making this world a better place. A patient person deals with much less pain, internal agony, and anger. The stress level of an impatient person vs. a patient person is night and day. Is a patient person more healthy than the impatient person? Generally the answer is yes. Less stress leads to better health, lower blood pres-sure, and a much more relaxed disposition.

What type of impact does patience have on others around us? It is much more pleasant to be around a patient person. Patience allows us to evaluate a situation before making decisions.

Patience allows us to examine what we can learn from any given situation. Patience is caring and kind. Patience takes practice and consistent effort.

Try practicing patience - your life will become much more tolerable for those around you as well as for you!

# CHAPTER 42

## Moderation

MODERATION IS FINDING a balance in everything we do in life. It has never been one of my strong points. I have had excessive traits my entire life. It took a while, but I am now starting to understand that moderation is a good thing. It is important to always strive to do our best. But wanting more and more and more is a desire that can be very detrimental to us.

What does lack of moderation do to us? We are excessive at eating and we gain weight and our health suffers. We are excessive at working and our pocketbook may benefit, but other parts of our life decline. Relationships and those we care about suffer. We don't have time for others any longer. We miss out on some of the most impor- tant things in life if all of our time is spent work- ing. We find a new love in our life and we become excessive. We want to spend every moment with this person. The smothering that is now happening has a long term negative impact on the relationship. The balance in our life suffers.

How do we find a healthy balance? We must first recognize the areas where we are failing to practice moderation. Once we are aware of these areas, we can work on finding balance. We might realize we are excessive and our first reaction may be to change so drastically that we go to the other end of the spectrum. From all to nothing is not healthy either. Now we are being excessive in the opposite direction. Practice minor adjustments. "Roller coaster" lifestyles add stress to our life. Work towards moderation and life will reward you!

# CHAPTER 43

## A Lesson from Dad

MY FATHER HAD been deceased for over two years when he came to me in a dream. The experience felt quite real and ended up teaching me a very important lesson.

It was early morning as I lay in bed. I felt awake, but knew I was dreaming. My father appeared in my dream and held me in a controlling manner. It made me feel paralyzed. I could not move, regardless of how hard I tried. He then told me that he realized he was extremely controlling while he was raising me. He wanted to apologize because he knew it was not right. He then proceeded to explain the lesson I should learn.

I had been treating my wife the same way. My wife and I would play around and tickle each other. But being stronger, I would always need to go overboard. When it was time to stop playing, I nearly always had to push it fifteen seconds longer. At this point, it would not be fun for my wife. My father explained, "You are doing to her what I used to do to you." Controlling those who do not have an option to stop the control is not good. In reality it is a type of bullying.

After the dream, I immediately woke up. I still could not move for about thirty seconds. I pondered the lesson he had taught me. When I told my wife, she confirmed what my father had told me, yes – that is exactly how it felt from her standpoint. My lack of awareness did not allow me to see this view.

Positive changes and new levels of awareness in our life may come from many different areas. Be open to all the options – they may even appear in a dream. Always a work in progress, this life we live. Thank you, Dad!

# CHAPTER 44

## Black or White (or Gray)

I HAVE HEARD it said something can either be black or white. You can choose which side to take. I prefer the third choice most of the time. Many don't realize a third choice exists. What is this third choice? How about gray? We are so set in things being one way or the other that sometimes we forget it does not have to be an absolute. Without gray, progress would be difficult to achieve. Gray is looking at all the options and then making a decision with the best parts of both black and white.

Walls are built when something has to be exactly one way or the other. Walls are used to separate people, not bring people together. Media loves to only offer two options. Many times they will not tell the whole story of other options that may be viable. It seems the main goal is to get two sides vehemently disagreeing and arguing. The media has then met their objective. How about the responsible goal of bringing people together? How about doing the best possible thing for the entire human race? We seem to have lost this somewhere along the way.

Gray may seem to be giving in too much. If you don't get your fully desired package, you have lost the battle. This is not true. We are all in this together. We need to take our time and look at situations from every angle. We are intelligent enough to come up with the best possible solution. Many times both sides can benefit from the best possible solution. Remove pride and let's try and find the best overall alternative for everyone. Gray is a pretty good color!

# CHAPTER 45

## Open your Mind

PROGRESS IS HALTED and learning is virtually impossible when people have closed minds. A closed mind can lead to anger, frustration, and conflicts.

Many beneficial things can come from having an open mind. Where does learning take place? Learning takes place in the mind. If our mind is open, we are willing and able to learn. We can learn from anything. We do not have to agree with a principle or idea to still learn from it. Resolutions are achieved by slight adjustments from an initial idea until the end result is reached. To move from this initial idea, your mind must remain open to all options.

If people are not comfortable with something new to them, they may consider it "weird." An open mind does not judge or consider anything "weird." I prefer to use the terms unique or different, as the word "weird" promotes a negative connotation. If something is outside our comfort zone we often fear it. Some of the largest opportunities to learn will occur outside our level of comfort. This is how many solutions and technological advances have been developed.

Not only does the human race make positive changes and evolve when the mind is open, but the soul also benefits. Our lessons occur when we have an open mind, an awareness, and a willingness to change. Keep an open mind and look for learning experiences wherever possible – your growth will be enormous!

# CHAPTER 46

## Knowing the Facts

WHAT ARE THE facts? Facts are different for everyone. Perception plays a large role in our life. Two people may see something happen from slightly different angles. Their definition of the "facts" may be completely different. Yet, each person is absolutely positive they are stating the facts. Facts are really adamant views of what people believe they know. We can say facts are opinions we believe in so strongly that we assume them to be true.

People see things a certain way and then have a tendency to attach their own beliefs to what they see. This can create problems because rarely does a person know all the facts. We may think we know what is best for someone. How can we, without knowing all the facts? We don't know what another person has been through or how they may perceive things.

Our best option may be to realize that we never really know all the facts. Remember, the world was factually flat at one time. Then someone proved it to be round and the flat world was no longer a fact. Realizing that we do not know all the facts allows us to be much more understanding toward others. It is okay that we do not know all the facts and never will during our time here on earth. Following this thought pattern will allow you to look at things from more than one perspective. If you realize that you do not know all the facts, your life actually becomes much easier. You don't have to always come up with the answer, for the answer may just be one person's perception. Knowing the facts is not required!

# CHAPTER 47

## Practice

PRACTICE IS GOOD for everyone. We learn from practice. It gives us confidence and a comfort level. We can practice just about anything.

Doing something for 21 straight days develops a habit or breaks a habit. Practicing something 10,000 times leads to true improvement. I don't know if these statistics are proven, but they are interesting.

Does it matter how we practice? Yes, it does. Practicing something incorrectly can instill bad habits and makes it difficult to achieve our intended goal. Lazy practice can lead to complacency and hurt our forward progress. Good practice involves dedication, hard work, and striving to make our best effort at whatever we are practicing.

Practice does not need to be dull and boring. Be creative and make games out of your practice sessions. Instead of looking at the goal you are attempting to achieve, set mini goals you can reach as you continue to practice. Each time you reach one of these mini goals, it confirms the progress you are achieving through your practice and gives you a feeling of accomplishment. Realize that failures in practice will allow you to make improvements. You continue to learn as you travel toward your optimum result. Success achieved during practice reinforces the action plan you have put in place.

What can you practice? Plan on practicing everything you do. Practice on your relationships. Practice your work. Practice communicating. Practice being a better person and adding positive energy and love to the world. If you make it fun, practice can be rewarding. As you continue to practice, the consistent progress you make towards your goal will come very quickly!

# CHAPTER 48

## Meditation

LIFE CAN TAKE a toll on us. The hectic pace can wear us down. Meditation is an opportunity to dig deep within ourselves and regroup. We can use meditation to escape the world around us and to recharge our internal batteries.

With good concentration levels, meditation can be achieved anywhere at any time. The very basics of meditation begin with simply watching and listening to your breath. As you breathe in, feel the oxygen come into your body and rejuvenate you on every level. As you breathe out, feel your body, mind, and soul relax. Breathing in, you feel positive energy entering your body. Breathing out, you release all negative thoughts and negative energy from your body. Your mind becomes stronger and your body becomes stronger in conjunction with the mind.

Although meditation can be done anywhere at any time, there are certain locations that are more conducive to meditating than others. These areas will make meditating much easier. Any spot in nature that is calm and relaxing is a wonderful spot to meditate. This can be done while sitting, standing, or even walking. Another good area to meditate is a quiet spot at home where you are comfortable. Some people will mediate on the floor, in a chair, or laying in bed. Meditation during yoga can also be beneficial. Yoga stretches and relaxes the muscles and the body, while meditation allows the mind to relax.

Meditation allows for relief of the stress we all experience in life. The relaxing results it provides is invaluable in this day and age. Give meditation a try and see what benefits are in store for you!

# CHAPTER 49

## Vibrational Frequencies

THE WORLD IS made up of many different frequencies of vibrations. A good analogy is radio stations. We tune our radio from one spot on the dial to the next and different sounds come through. We cannot see these frequencies, but they are there. Other dimensions are here with us in this world. They are just on different vibrational frequencies that do not allow us to see them.

Higher vibrational frequencies tend to be closer to the soul level. Lower vibrational frequencies tend to be closer to the human side. Higher vibrational frequencies increase our energy level and improve our well being, while lower vibrational frequencies decrease our energy level and have a negative impact on our well being.

There are ways people can increase or decrease their own vibration levels. Anger, guilt, resentment, medicine, junk food, electrical power lines, sugar, radiation, antibiotics, alcohol, toxins from our environment, yelling, screaming, arguing, and toxic negative thoughts are just a few things that will lower your vibration level. Love, joy, gratitude, forgiveness, acceptance, awareness, pets, nature, laughing, smiling, meditation, yoga, relaxing music, sunshine, outdoors, and healthy foods are just a few things that will raise your level of vibration.

Have you ever heard of a singing bowl? It is a bowl that can generate a very high pitched sound caused by vibration. It is said that meditating while using a singing bowl can raise your vibrational frequency to the next level. Some feel this can help in crossing to another dimensional level, which may allow us to communicate with those on the other side. Using a singing bowl can also raise the positive energy level to assist in transferring healing and positive thoughts to others.

How is your vibrational frequency? If you desire to work on it, you can always increase its level. Happiness and fulfillment will follow you as your vibrational level continues to improve!

# CHAPTER 50

## Three Steps to Solving a Problem

THERE ARE MANY problems in our world today. How is a problem solved if people feel a situation needs to be addressed?

The first step is awareness. When protestors take to the streets, they have signs and talk to reporters to express their side of the story and therefore awareness of the issue is being achieved. But many of the bandwagon protestors seem to miss the next two steps of the process.

The second step to solving the problem once awareness has taken place is to present a legitimate solution. This does not mean a one-sided solution that cannot and will not be accepted. It means a solution that has the potential to work out for everyone. Speaking to those and acting out towards those who have no power to control the intended result is fruitless. This only creates walls and hinders the opportunity for a solution. Getting the correct people to present a solution and getting the correct people to listen to a solution is key. Then negotiation is required to agree upon a solution.

Once a solution is agreed upon, the final step is to initiate an action plan to get the solution in place. Both sides must work together to accomplish the intended goal. Small adjustments may be required as the action plan takes place. With both sides working together the needed improvements and optimum result may be achieved. Communication is an important part in the entire process.

A friend of mine was caught up in a protest recently when traffic was stopped due to the protestors. He was interested in hearing what they were protesting and what they were looking to achieve. Unfortunately, what he experienced changed his perception and he had no interest in helping these people at all. One of the protestors flashed a strobe light from his cell phone in my friends eyes. Another one pounded aggressively on his windshield and he was forced to roll up his window and get out of the area as quickly as possible. Needless to say, he was not going to help these people and their cause. The protestor's actions created much more damage than good.

Negative energy, violence, and anger at these protests become contagious and spread like wild-fire. Constructive communication cannot occur in this type of environment. The protestors have become part of the problem instead of part of the solution.

If you believe in something strongly enough, stand up for it. Make sure you have the three step plan in place before you take it to the public. Awareness, a viable solution, and an action plan will help you achieve your desired results!

# CHAPTER 51

## Faith

THIS IS A big one! To have faith means to believe strongly in something that does not require physical proof. Why is faith so important for anyone? Faith allows us to deal with the toughest things in life. With faith, we can cope with disasters, tragedies, and negative situations. Without faith, we may not have the capability to handle some of these issues. Hope is similar, but in hoping we are wishing for something. With faith, we truly believe with our whole heart in something. Do you and I have a purpose for being here in this lifetime? I think we do. My faith in the Source of love and the afterlife allows me to believe in my purpose.

I see miracles happen every day – small ones, big ones, and those in between. Every life is a miracle. This perception strengthens my faith every day of my life. I cope with the death of ones I love dearly. I have faith that I will see them again when my time comes to leave this body. My willingness to be open to anything and everything allows my faith to grow stronger throughout my lifetime.

Faith is not a requirement for everyone, but faith will make your path much easier to travel. There are few negatives to having faith, but the positives are many. This is a choice that no one can take away from you – allow faith to be part of your life!

# CHAPTER 52

## The Human and the Soul

THE HUMAN AND the soul must find a way to work together in this lifetime. We are all souls here in a human body, not humans here with a soul attached.

Sometimes it is difficult for the human and the soul to co-exist. Human needs differ from the requirements of the soul. The ego has no part in the soul, but the ego dominates the human side. How can we allow both our human side and our soul to co-exist?

Let's start by looking at this from the human perspective. Some humans do not care to get in touch with their soul. Human desires rule their life and the soul seems to be non-existent. In this case, human successes such as monetary rewards or physical advantages are the main priority. What suffers? The heart and the soul suffer from this one sided lifestyle. Generally this person has deep internal battles which cause their life to be extremely miserable and unfulfilling. This person's misery can be greatly reduced if they give their heart and soul some attention. When wrapped into this human existence, awareness of the soul is frequently overlooked. The person continues to struggle internally without knowing how to overcome the issues they feel deep within. These people often find awareness on their deathbed. At that point, they realize all the things in material form cannot be taken with them. Those that figure this out earlier in their lifetime make great strides in opening up their heart and soul. They realize that life on earth is a blessing and they continue to grow and learn in all aspects of their life. Their soul benefits.

It is not an easy journey for the older soul or deeper soul who is trying to deal with the human side, either. This soul sees all the negative energy occurring in this world and may become introverted, avoiding human interaction. However, that is not why they are here. The aspects of soul must coincide with the human aspects and realize both are here to learn and grow. By avoiding the human side, the soul may actually limit or stunt the potential growth it is here to achieve.

We must all realize the human side and the soul are in this together. Acceptance of the path you are on is key. Grow and learn whenever possible. Allow your human side and your soul to enjoy the ride together!

# CHAPTER 53

## Rose Colored Glasses

THERE WAS AN article I saw on social media some time back telling of what a miserable place this world has become. It asked why anyone would ever want to live here. Generally, I prefer not to respond to social media as the drama that ensues is not healthy. But this time I made an exception.

I prefaced my comment, "This is just one person's view, but this is how I see it. Yes, there are many negative things happening in our world. But there are also miracles and positive things happening all over the world. When we get too absorbed in television and media events that are skewed towards drama and sensationalism it can have a negative impact on us. If we look for the positives, there are numerous ones we can find. Oftentimes, these positive things are found here in our own life. If we change our perception, we can create our own reality. This reality can be beautiful."

I received many likes and quite a few positive comments. On the flipside, I received two very angry comments. One of them stated, "How can you even consider thinking that way? Are you blind to the world? You are the problem in this world. It is people like you wearing rose colored glasses that just don't get it. Wake up and take your head out of the sand."

Well, at first, I was offended. This seemed to be a personal attack against me. Then I viewed it differently. I realized the person making this comment was upset and bitter. They were living a very difficult life. I felt compassion for this person and wished the best for them. But I refused to let their karma become my karma. I was in a good place. They were not. I was not about to change my views because somebody else was not happy with how I thought. I thanked the positive people for their comments and let the negative comments be. I guess, if I did reply to the negative side, I would want to say this. "Yes, I do wear rose colored glasses. I feel blessed that I am able to make that choice. You also have the choice of which colored glasses to wear. I feel sorry for you that you have chosen to wear such dark glasses. The darkness can seep into your heart and soul and lead to a very sad lifetime."

Yes, I do wear rose colored glasses and I like them a lot. Please don't be afraid to try them on – the view is spectacular!

## CHAPTER 54

# What if I Am Wrong?

HERE IS A question as we approach the end of the book. What if I am wrong?

Let's start with this question instead. What if I am right? If there is an afterlife and we are here to grow and learn this time around, how cool is that? I have found my purpose and I am living a love-filled life that is beneficial to both myself and others. I have worked at making improvements every day and every moment of my life. I have also attempted to help others make improvements and see things from a perspective that will bring them joy and happiness. This joy and happiness has been reflected back to me.

Now, back to the original question. What if I am wrong? What if there is no afterlife and we really do not have a purpose for being here? It's okay. Then I am still living a love-filled life that is beneficial to both myself and others. I have worked at making improvements every day and every moment of my life. I have also attempted to help others make improvements and see things from a perspective that will bring them joy and happiness. This joy and happiness has still been reflected back to me.

Either way it seems to be a "win-win" situation for me and for those around me!

## CHAPTER 55

# *What's Love got to do with it?*

# EVERYTHING!

# Author Biography

DAN BABCOCK SPENT his childhood and adolescence in Minnesota. He graduated from St. Cloud State University and later moved to the Minneapolis, Minnesota, area. He still lives there with his wife of twenty-five years, Debbie.

Babcock was inspired by his mother, Irene Babcock. She passed away in December of 2016, and he dedicates *Reflections: Words from the Soul* to her memory.

# Notes